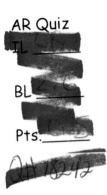

SUN

by Melanie Mitchell

first step nonfiction

Lerner Publications Company · Minneapolis

What makes the sky light
during the day?

The Sun makes the sky light.

The Sun is the center of our **solar system.**

All of the planets move
around the Sun.

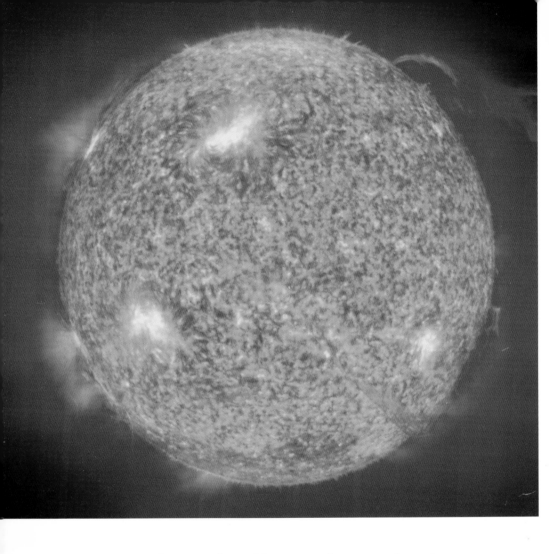

The Sun is the closest star
to Earth.

It is the only star we see
during the day.

People need the Sun for
heat and light.

Plants on Earth need light
from the Sun to grow.

People eat food from plants.

So the Sun also gives us
food.

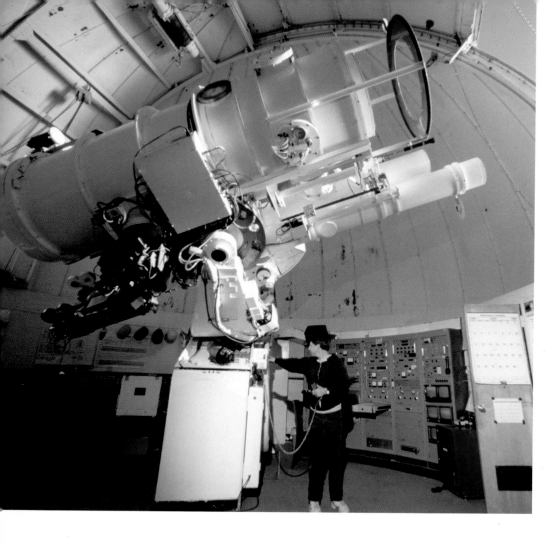

People study the Sun with special **telescopes.**

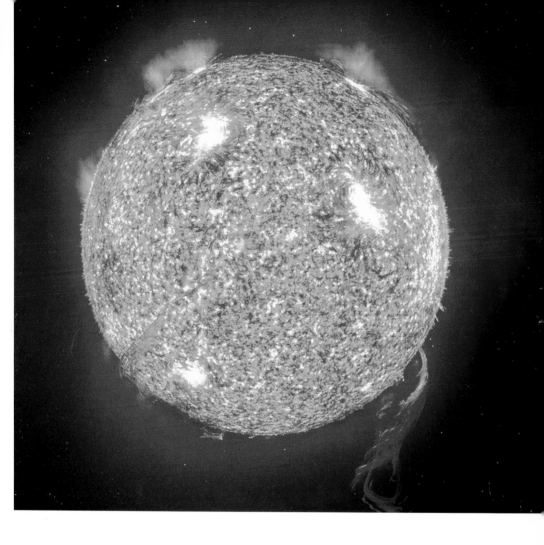

The Sun is made of very hot gases.

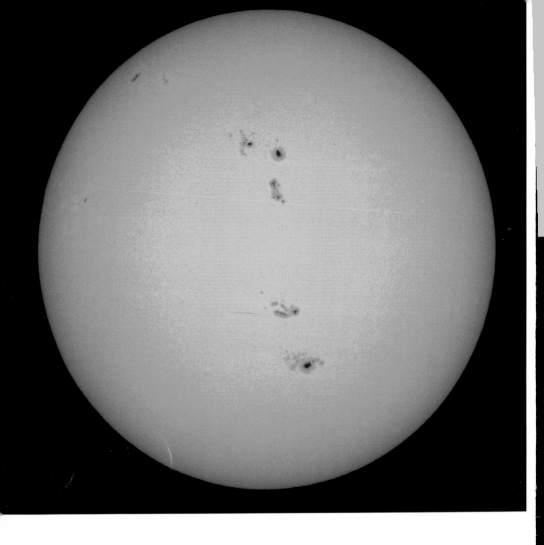

Cooler, dark spots on the
Sun are called **sunspots.**

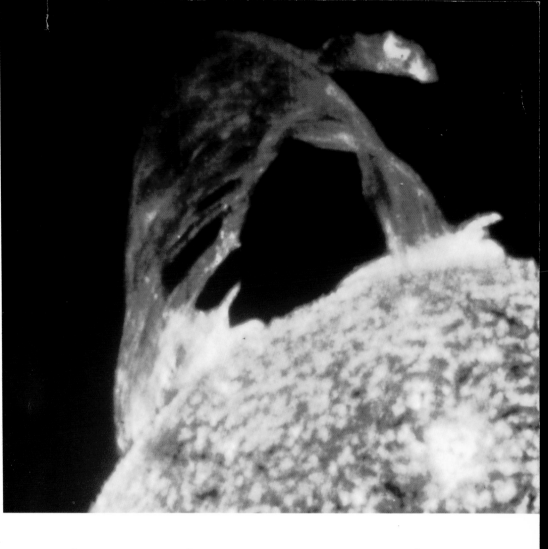

Loops of gases on the Sun
are called **solar flares.**

People wear **sunglasses**
when the Sun is too bright.

It is fun to play outside in
the sunlight.

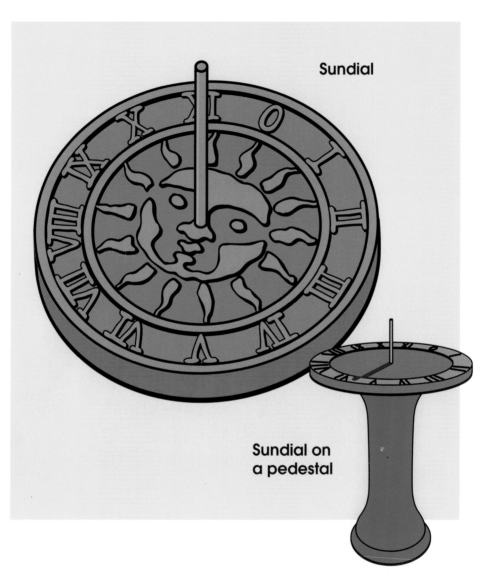

Sundial

Sundial on a pedestal

Sundials

Before clocks were invented, people used sundials to tell time. A sundial is a tool that can show what time it is by using the Sun and shadows. Sundials have pointers. The Sun shines on the sundial, and the pointer's shadow points to what time it is. As Earth moves and the Sun changes position in the sky, the shadow changes position and shows the new time.

Sun Fun Facts

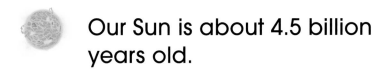 Our Sun is about 4.5 billion years old.

Our Sun is about 93 million miles away from Earth.

Light from the Sun takes about 8 minutes to reach Earth.

When the Moon passes directly between the Sun and the Earth, it is called a solar eclipse.

The Sun will continue to shine for at least another 5 billion years.

The Sun is a medium-sized star. It is a type of star called a yellow dwarf.

 The Sun is so big that one million Earths could fit inside it.

 The Sun is very hot. The temperature in the center of the Sun is at least 27 million degrees Fahrenheit.

Glossary

 solar flares – loops of gas that shoot out from the Sun

 solar system – the Sun, and the planets, moons, and everything that travels around the Sun

 sunglasses – dark glasses that protect the eyes from bright sunlight

 sunspots – cooler, dark spots that appear on the surface of the Sun

 telescopes – tools that make faraway things look closer

Index

The photographs in this book are reproduced through the courtesy of: © PhotoDisc Royalty Free by Getty Images, front cover, pp. 2, 3, 7, 8, 9, 16, 22 (middle); © Todd Strand/Independent Picture Service, pp. 4, 5, 11, 22 (second from top); © NASA, p. 6; © Agricultural Research Service, USDA, p. 10; © Roger Ressmeyer/CORBIS, pp. 12, 22 (bottom); © Novastock/Photo Agora, pp. 13, 22 (top); © John Sanford, pp. 14, 22 (second from bottom); © Science VU/Visuals Unlimited, p. 15; © Stock Image/SuperStock, p. 17.

Lerner Publications Company
A division of Lerner Publishing Group
241 First Avenue North
Minneapolis, MN 55401 USA

Website address: www.lernerbooks.com

Library of Congress Cataloging-in-Publication Data

Mitchell, Melanie S.
    Sun / by Melanie Mitchell.
        p.   cm. — (First step nonfiction)
    Includes index.
    Summary: A simple introduction to the sun.
    ISBN: 0–8225–5139–X (lib. bdg. : alk. paper)
    ISBN: 0–8225–3593–9 (pbk. : alk. paper)
    1. Sun—Juvenile literature. [1. Sun.] I. Title. II. Series.
QB521.5.M58 2004
523.7—dc21   2003005629

Manufactured in the United States of America
1 2 3 4 5 6 – DP – 09 08 07 06 05 04